Young Naturalist
Field Guides

Berries, Nuts, and Seeds

by Diane L. Burns
illustrations by John F. McGee

Gareth Stevens Publishing
MILWAUKEE

DEDICATION

To my dear daughter-in-law, Jill, who knows that everything grows with love.

ACKNOWLEDGMENTS

Many thanks to the following people for assisting in the research and proofreading
of this manuscript: The Rhinelander District Library, especially Cheryle Miller;
Rhinelander High School botany teacher Dawn Bassuener; Central Elementary School
teachers Tom Doyle and Joyce Minks; Consolidated Paper Company forester
Dan Hartman; Chequamegon National Forest wildlife biologist Norm Weiland;
field experts (and berry lovers) Robin and Jerry Burns; Bill and Barb Goosman;
and Clint and Jill Burns.

**For a free color catalog describing Gareth Stevens Publishing's list of high-quality
books and multimedia programs, call 1-800-542-2595 (USA) or
1-800-461-9120 (Canada). Gareth Stevens Publishing's Fax: (414) 225-0377.**

Library of Congress Cataloging-in-Publication Data

Burns, Diane L.
    Berries, nuts, and seeds / by Diane L. Burns; illustrated by John F. McGee.
      p. cm. — (Young naturalist field guides)
    Originally published: Minocqua, Wis.: NorthWord Press, © 1996, in series:
Take-along guide.
    Includes bibliographical references and index.
    Summary: Describes a variety of berries, nuts, and seeds that might be
found on a nature walk and includes identification information.
    ISBN 0-8368-2144-0 (lib. bdg.)
    1. Berries—Juvenile literature. 2. Nuts—Juvenile literature. 3. Seeds—
Juvenile literature. 4. Berries—Identification—Juvenile literature.
5. Nuts—Identification—Juvenile literature. 6. Seeds—Identification—
Juvenile literature. [1. Berries. 2. Nuts. 3. Seeds.] I. McGee, John F.,
ill. II. Title. III. Series.
QK660.B88   1998
575.6'7—dc21   97-51756

This North American edition first published in 2000 by
Gareth Stevens Publishing
1555 North RiverCenter Drive, Suite 201
Milwaukee, Wisconsin 53212 USA

Based on the book, *Berries, Nuts and Seeds*, written by Diane L. Burns, first published
in the United States in 1996 by NorthWord Press, Inc., Minocqua, Wisconsin. © 1996
by Diane L. Burns. Illustrations by John F. McGee. Book design by Lisa Moore.
Additional end matter © 2000 by Gareth Stevens, Inc.

All rights reserved. No part of this book may be reproduced, stored in a retrieval
system, or transmitted in any form or by any means, electronic, mechanical,
photocopying, recording, or otherwise without the prior written permission of the
publisher except for the inclusion of brief quotations in an acknowledged review.

Printed in Mexico

1 2 3 4 5 6 7 8 9 04 03 02 01 00

CONTENTS

Berries, Nuts and Seeds

INTRODUCTION 5

Wintergreen 6
Juniper 7
Cranberry 8
Bayberry 9
Currant 10
Sumac 11
Gooseberry 12
Raspberry 13
Wild Strawberry 14
Blueberry 15

MAKE SOME BERRY WATERCOLORS 16

Sycamore 18
Beechnut 19
Pecan 20
Hawthorn 21
Hazelnut 22

Acorn 23
Black Walnut 24
Hickory 25

MAKE A NUTSHELL BIRD FEEDER 26

Milkweed 28
Dandelion 29
Wild Rose 30
Cattail 31
Thistle 32
Burdock 33
Dock 34
Maple 35
Tumbleweed 36
Touch-Me-Not 37

PLANT A SEED GARDEN 38

FOR MORE INFORMATION 40

Metric Conversion Table

1 foot = 0.3048 meter
1 inch = 2.54 centimeters
1 pound = 0.4536 kilogram
1/2 cup (dry) = 115 grams
1/4 cup (liquid) = 60 milliliters
1 ton = 0.9072 metric ton

INTRODUCTION

Berries, nuts and seeds are actually the fruits of many kinds of plants. They come in many shapes and sizes and usually ripen near the end of summer. Most provide important food for different kinds of animals. Some, but not all, can also be eaten by people.

Depending on the kind of plant, its fruit may be juicy, or tough, or have hard shells. Usually, an outer covering protects the fruit from heat and cold, too much or too little moisture, and other dangers.

Plants protect their fruit in other ways, too. They may grow spines and thorns. They may taste bad or be poisonous. They may hang out of reach.

Berries, nuts and seeds can fall to the ground and begin to grow. They might also travel and start new plants far away. Some are blown by the wind. Some ride piggyback by sticking to fur or to skin. Some even roll along the ground.

This *Young Naturalist Field Guide* and its activities will help you identify some of the interesting things growing on plants, trees, and bushes. Use the ruler on the back cover to measure what you discover. Bring a pencil and notebook along to draw what you see.

Have fun exploring the world of berries, nuts, and seeds!

WINTERGREEN

WHAT IT LOOKS LIKE

Wintergreen is a short, creeping plant with a stiff stem. It grows from 4 to 6 inches tall.

The oval leaves are thick and leathery. They are dark green and shiny on top. The leaves grow from 1 to 2 inches long.

Wintergreen flowers are tiny and white, and they look like little bells.

The berry is the size of a pea and bright pink-red. It looks and feels waxy. Wintergreen berries ripen in autumn and stay on the plant all winter.

WHERE TO FIND IT

In dry, shady places look under large shrubs and pine trees. Look along roadsides, too.

In summer, look for the white flower. In autumn and winter, look for the bright pink-red berry.

Wintergreen grows in the eastern states and as far south as Georgia. It also grows in the north-central United States, west to Minnesota.

WHAT EATS IT

Wintergreen berries are food for partridge, grouse, deer, mice and bears.

INTERESTING FACTS

Wintergreen's nick-name "teaberry" comes from early settlers and Native Americans who made the leaves into a hot drink.

Early American families chewed wintergreen berries to freshen their breath.

Tell an adult where you are going, or take one with you!

JUNIPER

WHAT IT LOOKS LIKE

Some junipers grow as shrubs only a few feet tall. Junipers can also be short trees up to 40 feet tall. The bark is red-brown. Some kinds of juniper bark are soft and look shredded. Other kinds are very thin.

Some juniper leaves are needle-like and grow less than 1 inch long. Others are even shorter and scaly. They lay flat against the twig.

The berry is really a cone of plump scales. It is round and less than 1/2 inch across. It is green in spring and turns blue-black as it ripens in September and October.

WHERE TO FIND IT

Look for junipers in dry, rocky soil where other trees do not easily grow. They also grow on hillsides and in fields.

In winter, look for the blue-black berries still hanging on the branches.

Junipers are found from New England across the Midwest and south to Georgia, and from Texas into the southwestern states and north into the Rocky Mountains.

INTERESTING FACTS

Native Americans rubbed crushed juniper berries on their skin as an insect repellent.

A fully grown juniper can produce more than a million berries in a season.

WHAT EATS IT

Many kinds of wildlife eat juniper berries including turkeys, pheasants, quail, cardinals, robins, waxwings, finches, and woodpeckers. Mice, chipmunks, opossums, foxes and antelope also eat juniper berries.

Get permission before going onto someone else's land.

CRANBERRY

WHAT IT LOOKS LIKE

Cranberry plants grow from 3 to 6 inches tall. They grow on a creeping, woody vine. The plants look like a mat across the ground.

The green leaves are smaller than your fingernail. They are oval and tough.

Cranberry flowers are small, drooping, and pink-white. They bloom in May and June.

The oval berries are the size of marbles. The unripe fruit is green. It turns bright red in September and October.

WHAT EATS IT

Cranes and grouse eat cranberries. So do bears and deer. People eat cranberries, too.

WHERE TO FIND IT

Cranberries grow where there is lots of sunshine. Look in open edges along road-sides and wet places.

Cranberries grow from Massachusetts south to North Carolina and west into Minnesota. They also grow in Washington and Oregon.

Watch where you step.

INTERESTING FACTS

Cranberry's nick-name is "bear berry" because early settlers often saw bears eating this fruit.

More than 400 million pounds of cranberries are harvested every year in North America.

BAYBERRY

INTERESTING FACTS

A bayberry contains wax and is nicknamed "waxberry."

The leaves of bayberries smell good and are often used to scent candles.

WHAT IT LOOKS LIKE

Bayberry is a shrub. It can grow to about 40 feet tall, but it is usually much shorter. The branches are stiff, gray and waxy.

The stiff bayberry leaves stick upright and are shiny and tough. They grow about 3 inches long and about 1 inch wide.

Some bayberry flowers look like caterpillars. They bloom in spring.

The small, waxy berries are gray-green or pale blue. They look like tiny beads and are smaller than 1/4 inch. They ripen in early autumn. They stay on the bush all winter.

WHAT EATS IT

Quail, swallows and vireos eat bayberries. So do foxes. Deer eat the leaves and stems.

WHERE TO FIND IT

Bayberries grow in moist places, like swamps. Wear boots when you are exploring for them.

Bayberry grows across New England and along the East Coast.

Be sure you show any berries to an adult before eating them.

CURRANT

INTERESTING FACTS

This berry's nickname is "skunkberry," because raw black currants do not taste good.

WHAT IT LOOKS LIKE

Currants grow on a bush or shrub that is from 4 to 6 feet tall. Some currant bushes have thorns. Others do not.

The green leaves grow up to 3 inches long. They have 3 to 5 big dents on the edges.

Currant flowers look like stars. They grow in drooping clusters and bloom in May. Up to 10 small flowers grow in a clump. They can be green, pink, yellow or red.

The berries are round and the size of peas. They have a papery brown "pigtail" hanging from the bottom. There are up to 10 berries in a cluster. They can be red, white or black.

WHERE TO FIND IT

Currants grow in sunny spots and in moist places near water. Look along creeks and streams. They also grow on rocky hillsides.

Different types of currants grow throughout the United States.

WHAT EATS IT

Currant berries are eaten by catbirds and robins. Chipmunks and ground squirrels eat them, too. So do some people. Hummingbirds like the flowers.

Wear long pants and a long-sleeved shirt to protect yourself from thorns and insects.

SUMAC

Sumac grows on rocky ground. Look for it on open hillsides, edges of trails, grasslands and along roadsides.

WHAT IT LOOKS LIKE

Different types of sumac grow throughout the United States.

Sumac can grow over 20 feet tall. Some sumacs have thick, hairy branches that twist. Others have smooth branches. The bark is dark brown-gray.

Most kinds of sumac have narrow leaflets about 4 to 6 inches long. They have teeth on the edges and are whitish underneath.

The yellow-green flowers grow in clusters. They bloom in June and July. Each small flower has 5 petals.

The fuzzy berries are green and ripen to dark red. Each berry is the size of a small, flat pea. They grow in clusters about as long as your hand. The cluster looks like an upside-down cone.

WHAT EATS IT

Sumac berries are eaten by bluebirds, cardinals, thrushes and wild turkeys. Rabbits and chipmunks eat them, too.

INTERESTING FACTS

One type of sumac, the "staghorn," gets its name from the velvety twigs that look like deer antlers.

Stay away from sumacs that grow in wet places and have smooth, white berries—they are poisonous!

SPECIAL WARNING

11

GOOSEBERRY

WHAT IT LOOKS LIKE

Gooseberry shrubs grow from 3 to 5 feet tall. The stems grow every which way.

Gooseberry leaves are about 1 inch wide and 3 inches long. They have 3 to 5 large dents and large teeth on the edges. The green leaves are stiff.

The flowers grow in groups of 1 to 3 and bloom in April and May. They are small and shaped like a bell, and can be green, white, yellow or purple.

The berries grow in clusters of 1 to 3. The skin can be smooth or hairy. They ripen in late July and August. Ripe gooseberries can be green, pink or brown-purple. Some types have light colored stripes from top to bottom.

WHERE TO FIND IT

Gooseberries grow on wooded hillsides and dry ditches. They also grow in open woods.

Gooseberries are found from New England south to the Gulf Coast. They also grow westward across the Plains and the Rocky Mountains into the Pacific Northwest.

WHAT EATS IT

Hummingbirds like gooseberry flowers. Blue jays, chipmunks, skunks and mice eat the fruit. People eat gooseberries, too.

INTERESTING FACTS

The bottom of the gooseberry is really the top. The brown "pigtail" is what is left of the flower.

Gooseberries usually have thorns on the stems, especially near the branches.

RASPBERRY

WHAT IT LOOKS LIKE

Bushy raspberry plants grow 4 to 6 feet tall. The stems are thick and have prickles on them.

Red raspberry stems are brownish. Young black raspberry stems are green-blue. Older ones are red.

Raspberry leaves are medium green. They are silver-white underneath and about the length of your finger.

The flowers bloom in June and July in clusters of white or pink blossoms. They have 5 petals. The flowers are less than 1 inch wide.

Each raspberry fruit looks like a tiny round igloo. It is about the size of your fingertip. The fruit is green before it ripens to bright red or purple-black. Raspberries are ripe in July and August.

INTERESTING FACTS

Raspberry is sometimes nick-named "thimble-berry" because the picked berry looks like a thimble.

WHERE TO FIND IT

These berries like sunshine. Raspberries often grow in a thick tangle on the edges of woods, meadows and roadsides.

Raspberries grow across the northeastern and central United States and west into the Rocky Mountains.

WHAT EATS IT

Robins, bluebirds, flycatchers, sparrows, thrushes, pheasants, cardinals, catbirds and quails eat raspberries. Bears, marmots and people also like these berries. Rabbits and deer eat young raspberry stems.

The stems have lots of prickles! Be careful.

SPECIAL WARNING

WILD STRAWBERRY

WHAT IT LOOKS LIKE

Strawberry plants are short. They grow from 3 to 12 inches tall. The stem is hairy.

The leaves grow in threes. They are each about 1 1/2 inches long. They are deep green on top and light green underneath. Both sides can be hairy. The leaf tops have lines running from end to end. The edges have big teeth.

Strawberry flowers are always white. They have 5 petals and a yellow center. They bloom from May to September. The flower is the size of a dime and grows on a stem separate from the leaves.

The single berries are as small as the tip of your finger. Unripe fruit is green. Ripe fruit is bright red and shaped like tiny toy tops. The fruit ripens from spring to autumn.

WHERE TO FIND IT

Strawberries grow in sandy soil and lots of sun. Look for them in open fields and along roadsides. They also grow in the edges of open woods and meadows.

Wild strawberries grow from Maine south to Florida, and west to Oklahoma. They also grow from Alaska south to New Mexico.

WHAT EATS IT

This fruit is eaten by quail, grosbeaks, crows, waxwings, robins, deer, chipmunks and squirrels. Rabbits eat the leaves.

Interesting Facts

The name of this fruit may come from a long-ago practice of stringing the berries on lengths of straw to sell at the market.

Use a wide bucket for berries so they don't get crushed.

BLUEBERRY

INTERESTING FACTS

Blueberries were once used to dye the navy blue clothes of New England fishermen.

Early settlers believed blueberry syrup reduced fevers.

WHAT IT LOOKS LIKE

Short blueberry shrubs grow from 1 to 3 feet tall. The highbush blueberry can grow to 12 feet tall.

The leaves on some kinds of blueberry bushes are dark green with narrow, oval leaves from 1 to 3 inches long. Others are shiny light green, less than 1 inch long, and are very thin.

The flowers are pink-white, and grow in small clusters. They are small and look like bells. Blueberry flowers bloom in May and June.

The fruit is round and the size of a pea. Unripe fruit is green. Ripe fruit is pale blue to blue-black. It ripens in July and August.

WHERE TO FIND IT

Blueberries grow in sandy soil with sunshine. Look in open places like slopes and wood edges.

Different kinds of blueberries grow throughout most of the United States, except in the Desert Southwest.

WHAT EATS IT

Many kinds of wild animals like blueberries: bluebirds, thrushes, kingbirds, grouse, flycatchers, cranes, chipmunks, squirrels, deer, foxes, opossums and bears. People eat blueberries, too.

Wear old clothes. Berry juice can stain.

15

MAKE SOME BERRY WATERCOLORS

You can make watercolor paint with the berries you find (or buy at the store). Make several different kinds so your picture will be more colorful. You can even try mixing two kinds together to make a new color!

WHAT YOU NEED

- Newspaper to protect your work area

- An apron to protect your clothes

- A fine-line black magic marker or pen

- Watercolor art paper

- 1/2 cup of fresh berries, or frozen ones that have been thawed for each color of paint. Softer berries work best (like strawberries, blueberries, or raspberries).

- 1/4 cup of water for each type of berry

- A potato masher or a fork

- A small bowl

- A small strainer

- A clean paintbrush

- A glass with water in it for rinsing the paintbrush

- One small plastic tub for each type of berry used

WHAT TO DO

▼

1 Cover your work area with the newspaper and put on the apron.

2 Using the magic marker or pen, draw a picture on the watercolor art paper. Set it aside to dry.

3 Put 1/2 cup of one type of berries into the bowl and add 1/4 cup water.

4 Mash with the potato masher until everything is juicy.

5 Set the strainer across the top of the tub. Strain the juice through it and into the tub. This is the berry watercolor.

6 Repeat the water, mashing and straining steps with the other types of berries.

7 Dip the paintbrush into one of the berry colors and brush it across a part of your picture. (Hint: Watercolors look best when you do not try to stay inside the lines).

8 Then, rinse the paintbrush in the water and try another watercolor.

9 When you are finished painting, let your picture dry.

10 Throw away any extra watercolors.

When it is dry, hang your "berry" wonderful picture on the wall!

SYCAMORE

INTERESTING FACTS

The sycamore is nicknamed "buttonball" for the shape of its spiky fruit.

Long ago, canoes were made from the trunks. One of these was 65 feet long and could carry more than 4 tons!

WHERE TO FIND IT

Sycamores need lots of water. Look for them in the moist soil of woods and fields. They also grow in valleys and along wet bottomlands near streams.

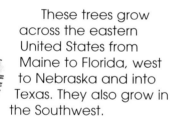

These trees grow across the eastern United States from Maine to Florida, west to Nebraska and into Texas. They also grow in the Southwest.

WHAT IT LOOKS LIKE

Sycamore trees grow to be about 100 feet tall. The bark is flat and gray. Big patches flake off, leaving behind bare, white spots.

The leaves grow up to 10 inches across. Each leaf has 3 to 5 large dents in the edges. They are shiny green on top, and light green and hairy underneath.

Sycamore seeds produce a hairy, brown, spiky-looking fruit that hangs on the tree all winter. It is about the size of a golf ball.

WHAT EATS IT

Finches and some squirrels eat sycamore fruit. Muskrats and beavers chew the bark and deer eat the twigs.

Take your time and do not hurry.

BEECHNUT

WHAT IT LOOKS LIKE

The beech is a slender tree that can grow over 100 feet tall. The bark is smooth and gray. It may have dark blotches and bands.

The oval leaves are 3 to 5 inches long. They are pointed and tough, with big teeth. The leaves are pale green to blue-green.

The fruit is inside a prickly, four-sided shell about the size of a grape. Two triangle-shaped, shiny brown nuts are inside. When ripe, the four sides of the shell curl up and the nuts drop to the ground.

WHERE TO FIND IT

Beeches sometimes grow by birch and maple trees. Around the base of an old beech tree, the shallow roots may sprout to form a cluster of little trees.

These trees grow throughout the eastern United States, west into Wisconsin and south to Texas.

WHAT EATS IT

Beechnuts are eaten by ruffed grouse, wild turkeys, wood ducks, blue jays, titmice and nuthatches. Raccoons, squirrels, bears and foxes also eat beechnuts.

INTERESTING FACTS

Early settlers stuffed their mattresses with thick beech leaves for softness.

Do not go near any wild animals you might see.

19

PECAN

WHAT IT LOOKS LIKE

Pecans are tall, slender trees that grow from 90 to 150 feet tall. The bark is tan-gray with deep ridges.

The leaflets have fine teeth and are about 5 inches long. They are dark yellow-green.

The oval nuts have smooth brown shells and are about 2 inches long. They ripen in September and October in clusters of 3 to 12.

WHERE TO FIND IT

Look for the tree growing in full sun, not in the shade of other trees. It grows in moist areas.

Pecans grow in the South, from near the Atlantic Coast west to Iowa and Texas. These trees also grow from Illinois south to the Gulf of Mexico.

WHAT EATS IT

Squirrels, chipmunks, and raccoons eat pecan nuts. Blue jays, woodpeckers, turkeys, bears, foxes, and people eat these nuts, too.

INTERESTING FACTS

A fully grown pecan tree can produce about a hundred pounds of nuts each year.

Remember to wear sunscreen and insect repellent.

HAWTHORN

WHAT IT LOOKS LIKE

INTERESTING FACTS

Hawthorn fruit gets its nickname "thornapple" from its shape and thorny branches.

Some Native American tribes believed that eating hawthorn fruit strengthened the heart.

Hawthorn is a shrub. It can grow to be 25 feet tall. The bark is smooth and dark brown. It breaks into thin, scaly plates.

The leaves are 1 to 2 inches long. They are shiny dark green on top, light green underneath, and hairy. There are not many teeth along the edges. Some kinds of hawthorns have large dents around the edges; others do not.

Hawthorn fruit looks like an apple that is less than 1 inch long. It is orange-red or yellow. There is one nut inside. Short, dry brown curls hang from the bottom of the fruit. The nuts ripen in September.

WHERE TO FIND IT

Look in parks and around homes. Hawthorns are planted in these places for their beauty. They are also found along fences and in fields.

In spring, sniff the blossoms. Most hawthorns have an unpleasant smell.

Hawthorns can be found throughout the United States except in the Desert Southwest.

WHAT EATS IT

Hawthorn fruit is a favorite of waxwings, sparrows and grouse. It is also eaten by mice, foxes, rabbits, bears and raccoons. Some people also eat it. Deer eat hawthorn twigs.

SPECIAL WARNING

The sharp thorns of this shrub can grow to be 4 inches long on the branches.

21

HAZELNUT

INTERESTING FACTS

This nut is also called a filbert.

Some people believe that holding a hazelnut branch helps them find underground treasures like water or minerals.

WHERE TO FIND IT

Hazelnut shrubs often grow in tangled, overgrown places, like roadsides.

Hazelnuts are ripe in August and September. Look for the shells which are different from other kinds of nuts.

Different types of hazelnuts grow throughout most of the United States.

WHAT IT LOOKS LIKE

The hazelnut is a shrub. It grows from 3 to 8 feet tall. The bark may be light yellow, or brown with tan spots.

The leaves have toothlike edges. The dark green leaves are shaped like hearts. They are 3 to 5 inches long and woolly underneath.

The dark brown hazelnut is round. Some kinds of hazelnuts grow inside a velvety, green case shaped like a comma. It is about as long as your finger. Other kinds of hazelnuts grow inside a tough, frilly shell in groups of 3 or more. All hazelnuts are about the size of a marble.

WHAT EATS IT

People like hazelnuts. So do squirrels, chipmunks, beavers, rabbits, grouse and woodpeckers.

22

Take this book with you and have fun!

ACORN

WHAT IT LOOKS LIKE

Acorns grow on oak trees. Oak trees grow to be 20 to 130 feet tall. The bark is gray-brown to dark brown. The bark has deep ridges or is flaky.

Oak leaves are longer than they are wide. They have uneven dents along the edges. White oak leaves have rounded edges without teeth. Black oak leaves have pointed edges and teeth.

Acorns are brown, round nuts inside a cup. They have a smooth, hard shell. Some kinds are as small as grapes, others are as big as golf balls.

WHERE TO FIND IT

Oaks grow in many places, such as forests, fields, swamps, and some dry areas. Oaks also grow around homes and along roads.

Oak trees grow throughout the United States.

WHAT EATS IT

Acorns are food for wood ducks, ruffed grouse, titmice, deer, mice, bears, squirrels and raccoons.

INTERESTING FACTS

An oak tree can make 1,000 pounds of acorns in a season.

Do not leave behind any litter.

BLACK WALNUT

INTERESTING FACTS

A tea made from the bark is used as a mouthwash by some people.

WHERE TO FIND IT

Look in open woods and valleys along streams. Black walnuts are also found in old fields and pastures. This tree often grows by itself. It likes sunlight.

In autumn, look on the ground for the dark brown shell with the nut inside.

Black walnut trees grow from Massachusetts west to South Dakota and Oklahoma, south into Florida, and west to Texas.

WHAT IT LOOKS LIKE

Black walnut trees grow about 120 feet tall. The bark is dark brown with ridges shaped like diamonds.

The leaflets are yellow-green and up to 5 inches long. They have teeth around the edges.

The nut ripens inside a shell. The shell is covered by a green husk. It is round and about 2 inches across. The husk turns dark brown in autumn.

WHAT EATS IT

Black walnuts are a favorite of many people. Squirrels, bears and raccoons also eat them.

Touching the brown husk will stain your hands and clothes. Wear gloves.

HICKORY

WHAT IT LOOKS LIKE

Hickory trees grow more than 75 feet tall. The bark is gray, and shaggy or scaly.

The leaftlets are dark yellow-green with fine teeth on the edges. They are shiny on top. They are about 5 inches long.

The hickory nut grows inside a shell covered by a green-brown husk. It is about 1 inch across and dark brown.

WHERE TO FIND IT

Hickory trees are often found growing next to oak trees. Young hickory trees need shade. The older trees like open, sunny areas.

In autumn, the dark hickory shells split open, and the nuts fall out.

Hickories grow from Maine south to Florida and west to Texas and Oklahoma. They also grow from Washington south to California.

WHAT EATS IT

Grosbeaks, nuthatches, turkeys, and woodpeckers eat hickory nuts. Squirrels, deer, woodchucks, raccoons, and people also enjoy them.

INTERESTING FACTS

Some types of hickory bark were used in pioneer days to make green dye.

Do not put your hands into any holes in trees. They may be an animal's home.

MAKE A NUTSHELL BIRD FEEDER

Here's a fun way to use the nuts and seeds you collect,
and give the birds a treat at the same time!

WHAT YOU NEED

- Newspapers to cover your work area
- A spoon
- A small bowl
- Birdfood mixture, made from the recipe below:

    1/2 cup peanut butter

    2 tablespoons of beef fat or lard

    4 tablespoons of seeds gathered from: thistle, dock, dandelion, milkweed, touch-me-not and cattail (or birdseed from a store).

- Empty shells of black walnuts and pecans (You can get these nuts at the store if you want. Break them in half with a nut-cracker. Take out the nuts and mix them into the birdfood.)
- An old board, about 8 to 10 inches long
- Small nails and a small hammer

WHAT TO DO

1 Spread the newspapers over your work area.

2 Mix the birdfood ingredients in the bowl using the spoon.

3 Carefully nail the empty walnut and pecan shells to the board using the hammer.

4 Spoon the mixture into the shells and place the board outside on a window ledge or a tree stump.

5 Refill the shells with birdfood when they are empty.

Have fun watching the birds dine at your feeder!

MILKWEED

INTERESTING FACTS

The milkweed's name comes from the milky juice in its stems.

WHAT IT LOOKS LIKE

This plant grows from 1 to 5 feet tall. The stem is thick. Most types have a milky juice inside.

Milkweed leaves are thick and tough. They are smooth and oval and about 6 inches long and 4 inches wide.

The groups of flowers are white, pink or orange. They are smaller than peas and are rubbery. They grow only at the tip of the stem.

The round seeds grow inside seed pods. Each seed is attached to silky threads. The pods are gray-green and have a thick, velvety skin. Some types are bumpy and others are smooth.

WHERE TO FIND IT

Milkweed plants like open spaces and may grow in a patch. Look for them where they will not be crowded by other kinds of plants.

Look for the seed pods in early autumn. They burst open and spill fluffy white parachutes of seeds into the wind.

Milkweed grows almost everywhere across the United States. It grows in woods and swamps, fields and meadows, road-sides and vacant lots.

WHAT EATS IT

Monarch butterflies like milkweed. Goldfinches eat the seeds. Antelopes also eat the plant.

Walk carefully so you do not injure any plants.

DANDELION

INTERESTING FACTS

The leaves give this plant its name. Long ago, the jagged edges were called "lion's teeth."

In sunshine, the bright yellow flowers open wide. When it is cloudy or dark, they close up tight.

WHAT IT LOOKS LIKE

Dandelions grow between a few inches and 1 1/2 feet tall.

Dandelion leaves are smooth. The edges are deeply cut with triangle shapes. The flower's stem is hollow and has milky juice inside.

Each stem has a yellow flower. The flower has many thin petals and is about 1 inch in diameter. The flower eventually becomes a ball of white fluff. Each tiny seed is attached to a fluffy thread. The seeds scatter easily with only a slight breeze.

WHERE TO FIND IT

Look on lawns, fields, roadsides and meadows.

Dandelions grow across the United States, almost anywhere plants are found.

WHAT EATS IT

Bees, and some flies and spiders like the flowers. Goldfinches, siskins, sparrows, grouse and pheasants gobble the seeds. Rabbits, deer, porcupines and gophers like to eat the plants. People sometimes eat young dandelion leaves as salad or dry the root and grind it up to drink like coffee.

The milky juice inside dandelion stems can be harmful if swallowed.

29

WILD ROSE

WHAT IT LOOKS LIKE

Wild rose plants grow from about 1 to 5 feet tall. Some types of rose plants are bushy, others are not.

The oval leaves are as long as your thumb. They are shiny green and have teeth on the edges.

The flowers can be as big as the palm of your hand. They are pink, white, yellow or red. Each flower has a yellow center. Many roses smell good.

Rose seeds are hidden inside a round fruit called a hip that is left over when the flower is gone. It is hard and shiny orange-red. It is about the size of a grape. Several dry, brown curls hang from the bottom. When the rosehip dries up, the seeds fall out.

INTERESTING FACTS

A long time ago in Europe, hanging a rose over a table meant that all talk beneath it would be kept a secret.

The fruit of the rose is called a "hip." Rosehips have more Vitamin C than oranges.

WHERE TO FIND IT

In summer, the flowers grow along roadsides and fences, and in fields. In autumn, after cold weather comes, look for the bright red hips. They hang like ornaments from the rosebush.

Wild roses grow nearly everywhere in the United States.

WHAT EATS IT

Grouse, thrushes, cedar waxwings, squirrels, and mice eat rosehips. Antelope and deer eat the twigs and leaves. Rabbits chew the bark and buds. Some people drink rosehip tea.

Sharp thorns are found on most rose stems.

SPECIAL WARNING

CATTAIL

INTERESTING FACTS

The name "cattail" comes from the shape of the fuzzy flowers, which some people think look like cats' tails.

WHAT IT LOOKS LIKE

Cattail stems grow up to 6 feet tall. The whole plant is thin. The leaves are less than 3 inches wide. They stick up like ribbons and can grow 3 feet long.

Each plant grows two flower spikes. One is above, and is less noticeable than the bigger spike below it. The bigger one starts out green and turns dark brown. It looks like a large hot dog.

The seeds are cottony yellow inside the brown spikes. In autumn, the spikes burst open and the fluffy seeds blow away.

WHERE TO FIND IT

Look for green cattail shoots in late spring, when they poke out of shallow water. The brown, fuzzy flowers are easily spotted swaying in summer, autumn and winter winds.

Cattails grow throughout the United States in wet places such as ponds, streams, swamps and ditches.

WHAT EATS IT

Geese eat the seeds and roots. Muskrats also eat the roots.

Check to see how deep the water is before you step into it.

31

THISTLE

INTERESTING FACTS

Some people used to think thistle cured them of sadness. They also thought thistle was a charm against deadly diseases.

WHAT IT LOOKS LIKE

Thistle plants grow from 2 to 5 feet tall. The stems have many branches and can have thorns. Thistle leaves can be thorny, too. They are stiff and narrow. Some have deep cuts on the edges.

The flower is a green ball topped by a rosy-pink, purple or yellow-white tuft. It can be as big as 2 inches across. It blooms in summer.

Thistle seeds form on the flower ball after the petals dry up. The seeds are dark and thin. They ripen in late summer and autumn and are blown away by the wind.

WHERE TO FIND IT

Look for the plant in pastures and along roadsides, especially in sunny places.

Thistle blossoms grow at the very top. Look for the puffy tuft in summer and into September.

Thistles of some type grow almost everywhere in the United States.

WHAT EATS IT

Bees and painted lady butterflies like the flowers. Goldfinches, sparrows, and chickadees eat the seeds. Antelopes eat the plant.

Be careful not to hurt yourself on the thistle's sharp spines.

BURDOCK

WHAT IT LOOKS LIKE

Burdock grows from 2 to 8 feet tall. The plant looks bushy. It does not smell good. The stem is dark green and has ridges. The hairy leaves are shaped like hearts and can be as large as dinner plates. They are dull green on top and grayish underneath.

Prickly, rosy-purple flowers bloom in August and September. They are round and about 1 inch across. There are several flowers at the tip of each single red-brown stem. When dry, the prickly flowers become stickers, each about as big as your thumb.

The flat seeds grow from 1 to 2 inches long. They have one ridge. The seeds are dark brown. They grow inside the sticker.

WHERE TO FIND IT

Look in pastures, vacant lots, and along roadsides and fences.

Last year's stickers are easy to find on their stalks at any time of the year.

Burdock grows across the United States.

WHAT EATS IT

Some people grow burdock as a garden vegetable, and eat the young roots. Pheasants eat the seeds.

INTERESTING FACTS

Dried burdock flowers are called "stickers." If an animal or person brushes up against them, they hook onto fur or clothing.

An inventor got the idea for Velcro when burdock stickers stuck to his clothes.

Wear gloves to protect your hands.

DOCK

WHAT IT LOOKS LIKE

The plant can grow from 1 to 6 feet tall. It looks ragged and has many branches.

A dock leaf is shaped like a narrow shield. It can be up to 1 foot long. It is green-brown and rough. Some types of dock have leaves with curly edges.

The flowers are bright green and feel scaly.

The seeds are brown and pointed, smaller than popcorn kernels. Each seed has a papery wing around it. The wings are either round or shaped like hearts.

WHERE TO FIND IT

Dock grows almost anywhere. Look for it in vacant lots, on roadsides, in marshes and fields. Usually, dock grows in a patch.

Different kinds of dock can be found almost everywhere in the United States.

WHAT EATS IT

Juncos, geese, ducks, rails and bobolinks eat dock seeds. Grouse, pheasants and rabbits eat both the leaves and seeds. Deer eat the whole plant.

INTERESTING FACTS

Many years ago in England, people stayed away from dock plants. They thought magicians used the stems to cast spells on people.

Do not hurt any part of a plant with your hands or tools.

MAPLE

INTERESTING FACTS

Maple seeds grow in pairs joined at the seed end. Each looks like a helicopter blade.

WHERE TO FIND IT

Look in city parks, along streets and in yards for maple trees. They are often planted in these places for shade.

Maple trees grow almost everywhere in the United States.

WHAT IT LOOKS LIKE

Maple trees can grow to be more than 80 feet tall. The bark is silvery and smooth on young trees. It is dark gray-brown with flaky grooves on older trees.

The leaves are shaped like a hand and grow up to 1 foot long and wide.

Maple seeds have wings. Each small seed is closed inside a papery wing. The wing is tan and up to 1 inch long. Two seeds are joined at the seed end. The pair twirls to the ground in autumn.

WHAT EATS IT

Maple seeds are eaten by grosbeaks, grouse and nuthatches. Mice, squirrels and porcupines also eat these seeds. Deer eat the twigs and leaves.

Watch for changes in weather.

TUMBLEWEED

INTERESTING FACTS

"Tumbleweed" is the nickname of plants that dry up and roll in the wind to scatter seeds.

WHAT IT LOOKS LIKE

Russian thistle is a kind of tumbleweed that grows from 1 to 5 feet tall. It looks like a ball of mostly stems and slender, dark green leaves. The 1/2-inch-long leaves are stiff and have prickles on the tips.

The flowers are small, green-white, or pink-red. They bloom in July.

The seeds grow inside a papery cup. It is small and red and shaped like a toy top.

Late in the growing season, the plant breaks off near the ground. When it is blown by the wind, the seeds scatter to start new plants.

WHERE TO FIND IT

Tumbleweed grows in dry places, like fields and deserts.

The easiest way to find tumbleweed is to look for the dried brown plant ball. It blows across open ground or gets caught against fences.

Tumbleweed can be found in the western and southwestern United States, east to Minnesota and Illinois. It is also found throughout the South, and north to the Mid-Atlantic states.

WHAT EATS IT

Sparrows, pheasants, quail, juncos and larks eat tumbleweed seeds. So do gophers and mice. Antelopes eat the plant. If needed, tumbleweed can be cut green and fed to cattle.

Take drinking water with you.

TOUCH-ME-NOT

WHAT IT LOOKS LIKE

A touch-me-not plant grows from 2 to 5 feet tall. It usually has one thin stem that is light green.

The leaves are pale gray-green. The 3-inch-long leaves are oval with thick teeth on the edges.

Some kinds of touch-me-nots have orange flowers with red spots. Some have solid yellow flowers. Each flower has three petals and is shaped like an open sack. Thin green pods about 1 inch long hold the dark brown seeds. The seeds fall out when the pod dries up.

WHERE TO FIND IT

Touch-me-nots grow in wet, shady places. The plant often looks droopy.

Touch-me-nots grow across most of the eastern United States, south to Alabama and west to Oklahoma.

WHAT EATS IT

Hummingbirds like touch-me-not flowers. The tiny seeds are eaten by quail, mice and squirrels.

INTERESTING FACTS

This plant gets its name because the ripe seed pods burst open when touched.

The juice in the stems can be rubbed on poison ivy rash to help healing.

Touch-me-nots often grow near poison ivy. Watch out!

PLANT A SEED GARDEN

You can plant a seed garden in spring if you have gathered seeds the year before. Or you can plant in autumn right after a seed-gathering trip. If you do not want to plant your seeds in the ground, you can put soil in a large pot or bucket that has a hole in the bottom. Plant your seeds and put the pot in a sunny spot outside—in the yard, or on a patio or balcony.

WHAT YOU NEED

- A sunny, unused corner of your yard

- A shovel or trowel

- A rake

- A watering can, or a hose for water

- Collected seeds from sun-loving plants such as thistle, dandelion, milkweed, dock and wild rose. If you have a shady place, try touch-me-nots, too.

WHAT TO DO

▼

1 Be sure to get permission before you dig up a corner of your yard.

2 Use the shovel or trowel to dig up the chosen area.

3 Remove all rocks and clumps of grass.

4 Rake the area smooth.

5 Sprinkle the seeds across the raked area.

6 Cover the seeds very lightly with soil.

7 Water gently. Water again during dry times.

8 Be patient. The seeds may need a winter's rest before they sprout.

You will never have to weed your seed garden. Any weeds that show up will likely be welcomed as additional food by the birds and other animals!

For More Information

MORE BOOKS TO READ

The Backyard Naturalist. Craig Tufts (National Wildlife Federation)
Exploring the Science of Nature (series). Jane Burton and Kim Taylor (Gareth Stevens)
Flowers, Fruits, and Seeds. Jerome Wexler (Simon & Schuster)
How a Seed Grows. Helene J. Jordan (Harper)
How Seeds Travel. Cynthia Overbeck (Lerner)
Trees. Young Scientist Concepts & Projects (series). Peter Mellett (Gareth Stevens)

VIDEOS

Plants for Food. (AGC Educational Media)
Seeds Grow Into Plants. (MTI Film and Video)
Trees, Shrubs, Nuts, and Berries. (Wishing Well Video)

WEB SITES

www.azshops.com/Brittle/Nut-facts.html
www.ngpc.state/ne./us/wildlife/plots.html

Some web sites stay current longer than others. For further web sites, use your search engines to locate the following topics: *berries, bushes, nuts, plants, seeds, trees,* and *wildlife.*

INDEX

berries 5, 6, 7, 8, 9, 10, 11, 12, 13, 14, 15, 16, 17
black walnuts 24, 26, 27
blueberries 15, 16

dandelions 26, 29, 38
dock 26, 34, 38

fruits 5, 8, 12, 13, 14, 15, 18, 19, 21, 30

junipers 7

milkweed 26, 28, 38

nuts 5, 19, 20, 21, 22, 23, 24, 25, 26, 27

pecans 20, 26, 27

raspberries 13, 16

seeds 5, 18, 26, 28, 29, 30, 31, 32, 33, 34, 35, 36, 37, 38, 39
sycamores 18

thistles 26, 32, 38
touch-me-nots 26, 37, 38
tumbleweeds 36

wild roses 30, 38